AF317058

Kids Devotional

5 Minute Devotions for Kids

By

Eileen Nyberg

ADISAN Publishing AB

Content

Introduction

What do you think of when you hear the words God and heaven? Many times we see God as a true friend and heaven as His home. With God's home being one filled with goodness, it is no surprise that we work hard with our family and friends to create a world of love and joy on earth.

Of course, there are times when we face big challenges in our life too. Worries about doing well in school and helping out our family and friends can make us feel a little frustrated at times. Fortunately, God is always with us and can bring words of encouragement in all things!

Through the topics covered in this book, God's word will uplift and bring comfort to the challenges we may see. We will get to know and understand God more through His lessons, as told through stories in the Bible.

Additionally, as we read forward in the lessons that God would like us to understand, we can also gain the tools to not only do good for ourselves, but share that same wisdom with others.

Above all, we must remember that God's lessons are not made to be picky or tell us we can't do things but to help us with our goals. After all, His own plan is to see his children happy and well.

Who is God?

Scripture: "God is light, in him there is no darkness at all."

- John 1:5

At some time or another, you may wonder and ask yourself, "who is God"? God may have been mentioned through your parents, relatives, friends, and others in your community, but it can still be a hard subject to understand.

To put it simply, God is good, and we often describe His personality and morals as the true light. As a creator, He truly loves what He has made, so He is very protective of our safety from harm and darkness.

One big way God gives us advice is through His word in the Bible. There can be times when we can even sense God's plans being worked out!

He cannot speak to us directly, but will always help us find the answers to our problems by realizing Him in our world. He is a true friend, an awesome listener, and the best source of advice. As a whole, God is a being full of love and our biggest fan!

What did I learn?

God is light, hope, and friendship. We may not see him, but we can always find Him through His word.

What Does God Do?

Scripture: "He spoke, it was done; He commanded, it stood fast."

- Psalm 33:9

If you had the same duties of God, what do you think would be your daily tasks? In reality, God has many jobs and responsibilities that He must take care of daily.

Just as chores are important to do to help out your family, God's responsibilities or daily chores are incredibly important too. One of God's chores includes taking care of His family and every other part of the world that He had created.

No matter how busy He might be, God takes the time to listen to our prayers and help us work hard toward our goals of doing good.

We can usually feel that our thoughts are less worrisome after we pray, as God has lifted the weight off of our shoulders again. God is always reliable in completing His chores of taking care of us too, so we always know that we can follow His lead at all times.

What did I learn?

One of God's most important jobs is taking care of His creations by being our most reliable and willful caretaker.

How Can We Serve God?

Scripture: "Serve the lord with gladness! Come into His presence with singing!"

- Psalm 100:2

One big project that God asks us to take on is to serve him, but what does this mean? Fortunately, God has made each of us with our talents and unique abilities that can help us figure out how we can serve God.

Overall we can serve God and pay our respect back to Him in many ways. From working with friends to helping our communities, we must use our gifts from God as our superpowers.

With the help of God leading us, we can take the love that He had used to begin our beautiful world, and make sure it stays just as lovely for years and years.

From simple requests to more complicated situations, we never know what God may have us help serve Him by, but without your help, God's hopes would be much harder to complete!

What did I learn?

We can serve God and do good in his name in many ways.

Being Good Like God

Scripture: "Be kind and compassionate to one another, forgiving each other just as in Christ, God forgave you."

-Ephesians 4:32

There can be a lot of meanings behind the word 'good.' In movies, we see that a lot of the time, 'good guys' will work hard and honestly to beat the 'bad guys,' but what does it mean to be good like God?

Like in make-believe stories of heroes, God is a force of good in a world that fights against all kinds of bad actions. In this case, God is truly the ultimate good anything can be.

In God's own quest for doing good, He also asks us to join Him. Our scripture shows that God asks us to be kind to one another, compassionate, and even forgiving, just as He has forgiven us for our own mistakes.

God is always rooting for us to stay on the side of the 'good guys.' He understands that we make little mistakes while we learn, and that's ok. The best part is; through forgiveness, we have time to try again and encourage our friends to do better too!

What did I learn?

God is truly good and would love for us to treat others with the same goodness He has helped us.

Who is Jesus?

Scripture: "For God so loved the world, that he gave his only Son, that whoever believes in him should not perish but have eternal life."

- John 3:16

As we read scripture and are told the legendary tales of the Bible, one of the most important stories is that of Jesus Christ and his sacrifice.

As Jesus got older, he had many challenges to work against. As he performed those miracles, he was destined to, some had improved their faith, but others still persecuted him for calling himself the Son of God.

Eventually, those who disliked Jesus crucified him. Still, because of God's plan and the choice of a sacrifice for all others' sins to be forgiven, Jesus was resurrected and joined his Father in heaven not long after.

Jesus was a strong advocate for all people from all walks of life, asking God to forgive the sins of everybody who truly hoped for forgiveness. Through the good deeds and purity of Jesus, God had given us the greatest opportunity of repairing our mistakes.

What did I learn?

Jesus, God's son, was brought onto earth to help teach us from good and bad as true saviors through his sacrifice.

What Can Jesus Teach Us?

Scripture: " I am the way and the truth and the life. No one comes to the Father except through me."

- John 14:6

As the Son of God, Jesus had a ton of lessons to share with people during his time. When we learn about Jesus's life, we also learn of his ways of life that allow us to walk with God.

In Jesus's time, many people were not following God's rules as He instructed, so they were living in sin. Many were also suffering from the results of these sins. Then, Jesus showed everyone his way of following God, and the blessings that came with it.

After showing everyone how to be close to God, another major lesson is forgiveness and kindness.

Just as God is, Jesus may not be seen in person anymore, but we can always talk to him through our prayers. Through him, we can share what we need help with and become closer to God. Jesus loves to help us out, and all we have to do is ask!

What did I learn?

Jesus teaches us much about kindness, forgiveness, and being close to God. We can always follow his lead!

Sharing God's Word

Scripture: "He said to them, 'Go into the world and preach the gospel to every creature.'"
- Mark 16:15

When we hear God's word, we feel uplifted and hopeful. Our sad thoughts fly away and are replaced with happiness and excitement!

God knows we cherish and feel good hearing about His lessons, so he guides us to share them with others we know too. In many of the tales in the Bible, God's followers share His word for others to follow in His light.

From Jesus and his disciples, to the stories of Moses and even Noah's journey with the ark, they all had to share God's word to offer salvation, safety, and forgiveness to many other people.

It can be a big task to work on, but we also have chances to share the gospel! From inviting family and friends to events and holidays celebrating God, to even sharing lessons with each other or comparing them to our everyday routines, the Word of God is incredibly flexible to share.

Prayer :

Dear Lord, as I work on learning your word, please give me the opportunity to share your lessons too! You wish for your blessings to reach far and wide, and I would love to help with that goal as best as I can.

What did I learn?

We must share God's blessings and words with everyone we can!

God vs. the World

Scripture: "Set your mind on things that are above, not on things that are on Earth."

- Colossians 3:2

We know that God's ideas are always made for truth and peace, but what about ideas in the world? God has created us with the ability to think and make decisions, but people may sometimes make bad choices. Doing this can lead to even worse consequences, and keep us from the light of God.

Sins can show in many forms, and we live in a world that can tempt us in many ways. For example, there has probably been a time when we have all wanted the newest toy, game, or tech.

It isn't bad to wish for new things, but when it is always what we think about, we have to ask God if we truly need it and live by His guidance. In a challenge like this and many more, we can always ask God for help in guiding us to the right answer!

Above everything, we need to put God first in our decisions and actions. Even if it means we have to help, our friends make a good decision too. Everybody likes getting rewards for doing good, and God has the highest one to give!

What did I learn?

God understands we have temptations from the world, but hopes to lead us in putting Him first in all we do.

What is Worship?

Scripture: "Give thanks to the Lord, for He is good; His love endures forever."

- Chronicles 16:23

We hear the word worship a lot in church and at home, but what does it actually mean? In a nutshell, worshiping God means receiving His love and guidance at all times and giving thanks for all He does for us.

When we worship, we should put all our attention into talking with God. Our main goal is to speak to Him, after all! Most often, prayer is used to speak and share our feelings with God. Whether in a group or private setting, out loud or in our minds, we can pray to God, and He will hear us.

The more we worship, the closer we can feel to God too. Worshiping can be a very personal part of our lives, and sometimes we may even share stories with God that are really private. We start to notice more how much He is a part of our world and how much we can be of His.

What did I learn?

Worship helps strengthen our relationship with God. We can rest knowing God will always listen to us no matter how we worship.

Staying with Truth

Scripture: "Let us not love with words or speech, but with actions and in truth."

- John 3:18

"The boy who cried wolf" is one of the most common folk tales we are told growing up. In the story, a shepherd boy becomes bored watching over his sheep, so he tells all the villagers that a wolf is trying to attack them many times. Eventually, they do not listen when a wolf does show up.

Just as the boy should have been telling the truth, God wishes us to always stay with the truth in everything we do.

Sometimes we may feel tempted to lie, even in silly situations. No matter what, God takes lying seriously and does not like it. The truth can be hard to share if it is not good news at times, but the problem can get worse if we do not tell the truth. In the end, honesty allows us to receive forgiveness and the chance to fix and learn from our mistakes.

What did I learn?

It is always better to face the truth than lie and upset God or those we care about. The truth can be hard to tell, but it is necessary!

Practicing Patience for God

Scripture: "The Lord is good to those who wait for Him, to the soul that seeks him"
- Lamentations 3:25

It can be hard to wait for things we're excited about. From new movie releases to the latest games and technology, our world can have us ready to get the newest things with only a tiny waiting period.

When you start practicing a new sport or game, it is usually your first time, and you may feel disappointed that you are not as good at it as you want. With practice over time, you have the chance to grow and do better and better. After a short time, you may find yourself an expert!

When we are working on new skills like this, we must also practice patience, as our results will not show until much later. The same is with our prayers to God.

Above all, He does hear us, but for us to receive His blessings, we may need to be patient in what time they arrive, just as He is patient with us.

What did I learn?

God requires us to be patient for many blessings in our life.

Helping Others as God Does

Scripture: "Don't withhold good from someone who deserves it, when it is in your power to do so"

- Proverbs 3:27

The word "Good Samaritan" defines a person who does a good deed out of love without thinking of a reward. In the bible, Jesus tells a tale of a good samaritan traveler who had seen another who left on the road, hurt and robbed.

Although others did not stop to think of the hurt person, the samaritan did and could lend a hand out of compassion. As God wishes for us to love our neighbors, He also wishes for us to be active in lending a hand out to help if we can.

No matter how big or small we are, there is always a way for us to help each other. From doing chores at home and assisting our teachers in class to even helping a friend with their worries, there are plenty of opportunities to practice being our versions of a good Samaritan.

No matter how we help, it's always appreciated!

What did I learn?

Working together is important to God, especially when somebody needs help…and He loves when we try and help out too.

Understanding God's Lessons

Scripture: "Get wisdom, get understanding; do not forget my words or turn away from them."

- Proverbs 4:5

When we read and learn about the stories God tells through the bible, sometimes it can be hard to understand. There are many names, places, and even lessons to be learned!

To help with our journey through understanding God's word, fortunately, we have help available. From asking a grownup and reading extra devotionals to even participating in fun activities and games, there are many ways we can practice God's lessons and understand His words.

Finally, do not forget that it is ok to re-read verses or ask questions until they make sense. Everybody is different in how they start to understand God's lessons, so what may seem easy to you can be hard for a friend. God is always patient when it comes to learning His word, and even He would love to help us learn it!

What did I learn?

It can be hard to understand God's lessons, but the Bible and His word can help us in our journey.

Being a True Friend

Scripture: "Carry each other's burdens, and in this way, you will fulfill the law of Christ."

- Galatians 6:2

What do you think makes a true friend? God describes a true friend as selfless, lending a hand to anyone who needs it. Above all, God hopes for us to be true friends with everyone we know.

One big lesson that God teaches is that we must work hard to love everyone, even those we might not like or people that are being mean. It can be a very hard lesson to practice, but God explains that we need to act out of kindness and forgiveness just as He has for us.

Whether we are as close as can be or in the middle of a fight, God expects us to stand up for and care for all our friends every day.

God always reminds us that aside from the problem, big or small, there is always time to make things better, apologize, and make both old and new friendships stronger by offering a helping hand.

What did I learn?

Being a true friend means helping and loving selflessly, just as the Lord does to us.

God Never Changes

Scripture: "The grass withers, the flower fades, but the word of God will stand forever."

- Isaiah 40:8

As we grow up, change can be everywhere. A new school, new hobbies, and even new favorite foods can be something that can change as we accomplish old goals and start new ones. Many things can change through nature, too, such as the seasons changing from fall to winter and spring to summer.

Change in these examples can be good, but it can also be scary at times. Fortunately, we will always have one thing that will never change their support for us, God.

No matter the season or the changes in our journey, God will always love and cherish us. He helps us through the toughest and the easiest times in our life without thinking twice.

We often call God's will and rules constant, meaning they do not change either. We can always look back to His word for guidance, care, and reassurance.

What did I learn?

God will never change. He is always constant.

Learning from Mistakes

Scripture: "For the righteous falls seven times and rises again, but the wicked stumble in times of calamity."

— Proverbs 24:16

We are all human, and as we go about our lives, we can make big and small mistakes. From getting a question wrong on a test to accidentally breaking a family's things at home, sometimes our mistakes have consequences that affect us or others.

Fortunately, God understands that even though we make mistakes, we can learn from them. Sometimes we can even be hard on ourselves for our mistakes and forget the lesson God is trying to teach us through it.

No matter how difficult it may seem at first, we can always seek God's help to figure out how to fix our mistakes and even understand how to prevent them from happening again.

Mistakes are ok to make as long as we gain wisdom from them. God always wants us to do our best, so as you ask for His guidance in fixing our mistakes, you will find yourself doing better and better!

Prayer :

Dear Lord, as I make mistakes along my journey in life, please help me to remain true to your wishes and learn from them.

What did I learn?

We all make mistakes, and God expects this. The most important thing is we try to learn from them and do better in the future!

Keeping Our Promises

Scripture: "You have heard that it was said to the people long ago, 'Do not break your oath, but keep the oaths you have made to the Lord."

- Matthew 5:33

Have you ever experienced somebody breaking a promise? Promises can be about big or little things, but when broken on purpose, we usually feel down and wonder why it was broken.

Just like we feel when a promise is broken, God becomes disappointed when we also break our promises to Him. In all things, God keeps every promise He makes and, in return, asks us to do the same.

In all that we do, we should make sure the promises that we tell others are kept. God wants us to be of our word, meaning that if we say we are going to do something, we should be honest, try our very best, and work to be successful, just as we would like others to do for us!

What did I learn?

God always keeps His promises to us and remains true, so He asks us to do the same in all that we do!

Being Brave With God

Imagine you are about to dive far down into a pool of water. The longer you stand above it, the more intimidating it can look. You may even feel like giving up and climbing back down in times like these!

Fortunately, at all times, you have an incredible safety net with God. Sometimes things can start to feel scary, or you think you can't do something, but God reassures us that He is always there to guide us.

One of God's biggest promises to us is that of our safety. He asks us to be brave in our challenges because He knows we will be ok, even if we aren't sure quite yet.

No matter the circumstance, God is here for us, lending His own bravery for us to accomplish our goals. All he asks in return is for us to take a 'leap of faith' in His guidance…just like we would go on a diving board!

What did I learn?

God gives us the ability to be brave, even in the scariest of times, with His strength!

Using our Strength

Scripture: "The Lord is my strength and my shield; my heart trusts in Him and He helps me."

- Psalm 28:7

Just as we can ask God for help in our ability to be brave, God can show us how to be strong too.

A lot of times, we picture strength as related to our size of ability, but God recognizes strength in many different ways. Although the physical strength of our muscles can be important for some tasks, God also explains that our strengths can come from our hearts too.

Our ability to be compassionate to others, solve problems, and even realize when we must ask God for help can be a great strength that we must practice as well.

Overall, God can act as a big strength for us, too, as His words uplift us and encourage us through all times. No matter how we show our natural strengths, we can be assured God will help us with them, as our trust in Him can go such a long way!

What did I learn?

God not only gives us what we need to be strong but helps us realize our strength through all things

Keeping Peace

Scripture: "Blessed are the peacemakers, for they shall be called sons of God."

- Matthew 5:9

When God created the world, He gave us the tools to share His vision of peace and love through our actions. Peace is a very important trait to God because it sets a foundation for many other positive characteristics. Even as others may work against God's vision for peace, we must help add to the good side that assists God's word.

Once you start looking for ways to keep our world peaceful, you may find dozens of opportunities through God to do so! From sharing His love and understanding through positive words or actions in helping others, peace is found in every part of our lives.

Sometimes it may be hard to share ideas of peace with those who are upset or angry, so what can we do at these times? Fortunately, God offers to listen to us for the help of others, and we can always look to Him to help us know what our best choice should be in sharing His way of peace!

What did I learn?

As the greatest peacemaker, God wishes for us to carry and keep His peace on Earth.

God Carries Your Worries

Scripture: "Cast all your anxiety on Him, because He cares for you."

- Peter 5:7

What was something you were worried about recently? The challenges of our world can often cause stress or make us uncertain about what we should do. Fortunately, with the help of God's guidance, we can get help carrying even our biggest worries.

As we grow up, there are many things to think about, from what we want to do when we are older to even more recent ideas, such as what changes a new school year can bring. For these examples, these changes are exciting, but they can also make us nervous.

One amazing perk of having God with us anytime we need him is that He will always be here to listen to our worries and what makes us nervous. In this, God can give us peace and reassurance that we are on the right path.

What did I learn?

One of God's biggest promises to us is that He will always carry our worries. No matter the situation, He will help relieve us of our anxieties.

God Listens

Scripture: "Whatever you ask in prayer, you will receive, if you have faith."

- Matthew 21:22

Imagine all of God's duties from being the leader of Heaven and Earth. When you start adding them up, it sounds like God is very busy! Fortunately, God is the best equipped for the role. No matter how busy or how many people he may need to take care of, he will still listen to each of us!

Just as God listens to us when we express all our worries, He also hears our thanks to Him and even our wishes or dreams we want to share.

Above all, God has created each of us with our unique set of talents. As we continue to grow up to get better in those talents and even discover new ones, God is with us every step, listening carefully to share anything we may need along the way.

What did I learn?

God listens to our needs and prayers and our biggest dreams in life. He loves to help us succeed.

Following God's Plan

Scripture: " I will instruct you and teach you in the way you should go; I will counsel you with my eye upon you."

- Psalm 32:8

Almost every day, our teachers and parents plan what we will need to do for the day. From school to chores, we have to help at home, making plans to keep us on track to finish our projects and make more room for fun.

Sometimes, we may need help figuring out how to plan our biggest goals, but do you know God has a plan for us to help complete all that we do?

Ever since He created our world, God has made huge plans for each and every one of us. He hopes to help us accomplish our goals, but he has one plan for the big picture for us too.

God's biggest plans include caring for us until we return to Him in heaven. To do this, He tells us of all the stories and lessons He can to have us walk with Him in understanding. Eventually, through goodness, we will return to God through His plans!

What did I learn?

God has big plans for our lives that are good, so we must do our best to follow God's path of light and goodness.

Exploring Our World

Scripture: " It is I who made the earth, and created upon it."

- Isaiah 45:12

As God created our world, He did many wonders. From the tallest mountains to the deepest parts of the sea, our natural lands are incredible to see and filled with wildlife and beauty at every corner.

No matter where you live, God has created such a lovely diversity of flora and fauna. You may feel urged to explore it!

Whether you're on a field trip to a local park or on a family hiking trip, take some time away from the hustle and bustle of everyday life to explore what can be found in nature, as even the tiniest ants can be interesting as they go along their own work for the day!

As He created our world, we were given plenty of options to explore and see all God does for nature. We work hard to see all the good that God has made on our earth and care for it just as much as it can care for us through clean air, food, and peace.

Prayer :

Dear God, thank you for creating such a beautiful world for us to explore! I hope to always cherish and take care of it, just as you made nature care for us.

What did I learn?

The world God has made is full of wonders, big and small…we should take the time to explore and appreciate each and every one of them!

Be Generous

Scripture: "Good will come to those who are generous and lend freely, who conduct their affairs with justice."

- Psalm 112:5

Do you ever find it hard to share your own things? Lending out important things to others or giving our old things away that we don't use can be difficult!

In all circumstances, God wishes for us to be generous with both sharing and giving away our help and material objects. By being generous, we receive generosity from others in addition to God's blessing of doing good.

Being generous and charitable with the things we do not use or can have others borrow can make another person very grateful for the help. Just as God is generous in His promises to us, He wishes for us to share that generosity with each other!

Whenever we find it hard to be generous, we can ask God to help us find our patience and happiness with generosity..especially as He shows us all the good things that come from sharing!

What did I learn?

God is gracious in what He provides for us and, in turn, hopes for us to remain generous in our actions towards others no matter what.

Solving our Problems

As we grow up and have more responsibilities, we might have more problems to solve every once in a while. This can seem scary at first, but with the help of God, we can accomplish any challenges we face!

From solving problems at school with our homework to helping our family around the house, many problems can become easy to solve in a short amount of time, but others may be harder or take longer to figure out.

Even though some problems may be challenging to face, it is ok to turn and ask for help. Just as we can ask our parents, teachers, family, and friends for help if we need it, we can rely on God too.

With God's love, He hopes to give us the tools to solve any problem we ask Him for guidance.

What did I learn?

God lends us His strength to solve any problem we face. He knows what we can accomplish!

God Hears our Prayers

Scripture: "Call to me and I will answer you, and will tell you great and hidden things that you have not known."

- Jeremiah 33:3

From His word, we know God hears us through all things. He is with us through the good times and the bad times and offers His help all in between.

Of course, as we cannot physically see God while He is in heaven, we always have a direct call line to reach him through our prayers! God is a great listener, so whenever we call upon Him, He will answer.

God also gives us the option to pray in many different ways. You may often be asked to pray together in the church, for holidays, or before meals. We can also pray privately too.

When we pray by ourselves, we can share with God our biggest hopes, our challenges, and anything else that may come to mind. God's love for us encourages Him to listen and help in all things!

> **Prayer :**
>
> God, as far as I can remember, you have kept an open ear and mind to every one of my prayers, no matter how long or short, and for that, I'm eternally grateful!

What did I learn?

In times of both peace and trouble, God hears our prayers. He may even answer them before we have the chance to ask!

Honoring Your Parents

Scripture: "Honor your mother and father as the Lord your God commanded you."

- Deuteronomy 5:16

Our parents and guardians do a lot for us every day. From taking care of us as a baby to ensuring we have everything we need to learn and grow, God hopes for us to return the same kindness shown to us through respect and honor.

One big goal promised to God as a parent is for a mother or father to lead by example and teach us God's rules to help us walk in His light. In this, our parents show us honesty, compassion, and patience in learning.

Above all, our parents truly wish the best for us, so in return, we must offer the same respect for their rules or reasons for doing things…many times, if we don't understand and ask them why there is a good reason!

For God, respect and love go a long way. Even if it's something small like helping with chores or respecting God's rules, it's guaranteed that it will be noticed!

What did I learn?

We should honor our parents as God wishes, with respect and love, just as they give to us!

God Encourages Creativity

Scripture: "Whatever you do, work heartily, as for the Lord and not for men."

- Colossians 3:23

There is no doubt that God is a very creative being. God's creativity is unique from our natural world to each of us, making no two things alike!

Just as God is a master at creativity through His designs, He has given us unique talents that we can harness to be just as creative on our own time.

From becoming skilled at painting and design to be good with numbers or science, we all have something to offer to share with one another that can vary a lot.

Overall, God encourages us to work hard to explore our gifts, find what we are good at, and practice it where we continue to improve. Before you know it, you will share your talents with those around you just as God has!

What did I learn?

God is a creative being with all that is unique in our world. He would love for us to use our gifts of creativity for good too!

Love Like God & Jesus

The biggest message God could give us through His word and actions is His message of love. God's will is truly good, and with that comes His passion for sharing His love and encouraging us to love each other.

Through God's love, Jesus acted to save everyone who had sinned and required redemption. Just as his father did, Jesus could see the good in everyone without judgment and called for forgiveness.

In God's pursuit of complete peace, He asks us to love each other just as much. We should treat each other with kindness, no matter the situation, because it is healing for the other person and us.

Finally, we must never forget that in times that this may be hard, we can always ask God to help us in ways we can still show our love.

What did I learn?

God hopes for us to love each other just as we are loved…unconditionally and without hesitation.

Finding Silver Linings

Scripture: "Trust in the Lord with all your heart, and lean not on your own understanding."

- Proverbs 3:5

There's no doubt that bad experiences can get you down. Whenever negative things happen, we can feel discouraged and upset. Still, God can help us find the silver lining in even the hardest times.

Have you ever played a game where your team lost? It can truly feel discouraging, even to leaders and coaches. When this happens, you may often be told to look on the bright side or for a silver lining. In short, this means we should look at the bigger picture and our overall goals with God too!

Although you lost the game, that doesn't mean you can never win later. Even though today was filled with many challenges, it doesn't mean tomorrow will be. After all, sometimes, even losing or problem-solving those bad days helps you grow stronger and more capable of winning!

What did I learn?

When we face challenges, big or small, we should rely on God's wisdom for what could be next; finding the silver lining in a grey cloud.

Asking For God's Help

Imagine you are looking for a certain book in the library. This book is your favorite, so you know its name by heart, but this library is huge. You aren't sure where to start…what can you do?

In this example, you might think to ask one of the librarians. Surely they would be able to point you in the right direction! Just as we turn towards others who can help with our questions, we should also be comfortable with turning to God for help whenever we could need it.

In all things, we can ask God for any help or guidance we may ever need. He not only acts as our closest friend but is full of wisdom in all the answers we could ever imagine!

We are incredibly lucky to have God's help in so many parts of our lives, and we will always be there to fill in the blanks for anything we need help with.

What did I learn?

We can reach out for God's help anytime, and He will gladly listen.

Good vs. Bad

Scripture: "Do not be overcome by evil, but overcome evil with good."

- Romans 12:21

God's biggest lesson is that He teaches us good from the bad. Above all, He tries to guide us to make good decisions that align with His rules. Although this can seem challenging, it is much easier in practice with God supporting us.

We learn from God and our parents what good and bad behavior are at an early age. From ensuring we help out around the house to obeying laws such as not stealing, God often gives us similar rules to work on spiritually.

As you grow through prayer with God, you will continue your spirit of goodness. This means that on top of doing good actions,

God can help guide our thoughts, desires, and future decisions toward doing good. No matter what, God is always there to remind us how we can do good to uplift ourselves and others!

What did I learn?

God wishes us to fight for good daily by following His word.

Enjoy the Little Things

Scripture: " In everything give thanks; for this is the will of God."

- Thessalonians 5:18

There is no doubt that our world is busy. With so many things to do, including responsibilities and fun, there can be a lot to handle!

Of course, we must give thanks for the big events in our lives, but what about the small ones? As God has appreciated everything He has created or helped with, we should also appreciate the little things.

From big events in our lives, like birthdays and graduations, to smaller occasions, such as going out to grab a small treat or being able to be gifted the newest toy, we should stop to thank God each step along the way.

It is good to be thankful for the larger parts of our lives, but a lot of times, if we take a moment, we will notice that many smaller parts have built us up along the way!

What did I learn?

We should always be thankful for all our blessings, big or small.

Prayer Power

Scripture: "Then you will call upon me and come and pray to me, and I will hear you."

- Jeremiah 29:12

When do you like to pray? Whether in a group at church, with family or even privately by yourself, God is very flexible in the times we can speak to Him through prayer and is very adaptable towards our needs.

No matter how you pray, God always listens to our concerns, our thanks, and any other thoughts we would like to share with Him! God truly does care for our needs and thoughts, making time for what we may require now or in the future.

Especially as we use prayer to talk to God and He listens to our needs, you will find that God's promise of prayer is also incredibly effective.

Through prayer, He will always comfort us by taking our burdens and providing us peace of mind. In times of worry and peace, you should never forget He is always here for you!

What did I learn?

God not only listens to our prayers but speaking to God holds a lot of power!

Exploring Changes

When was the most recent time you experienced a big change? As time goes by, we go through many changes in our lives. A big move, entering a new grade, and even trying out a new hobby can bring big changes, but we are always reassured with God's help.

In the beginning, God had made the routine change a natural part of our world. From the seasons to the rise and fall of ocean tides, the land and all that live on it constantly change.

We also find plenty of changes similar to the earth in our lives. Still, occasionally these can be scary to go through. We may feel as though we don't know what to expect. Still, fortunately, through God's strength and reassurance, we can accept our changes as a new chapter in God's plan for us, with many opportunities ahead.

What did I learn?

God has created changes in all things; this can be scary, but God always supports us.

Keeping Good Friends

Scripture: "Dear friends, since God loved us that much, we surely ought to love each other"

- John 4:11

Spending time with friends is always cherished, but how do we know if the friends we keep are good? Or if we are good friends ourselves?

In all that we do, one of God's requests for us is to be a good friend to everybody. To be a good friend, we should work to be open, honest, and available to lend a hand, just as we would wish another to do for us!

Of course, there will be times when we might not agree with others, but we should still act friendly. It's ok to disagree, but it should never be met with a poor attitude. Even with those who are negative, our positivity can be contagious!

Just as God has loved us uniquely, both inside and out, He hopes we can keep and be good friends through the same love. In short, keeping good friends starts with being a good friend!

What did I learn?

God encourages us to keep good friends and be good friends by following His guidance in honesty, generosity, and kindness.

Help Your Community

God has given us many gifts in our lives, and the most important is our ability to make friendships and communities. In this, God has our support, and we care for one another, encouraging each other along the way.

Just as God has asked us to be good friends, He hopes for us to take care of our community. Participating in group events, volunteering, and even working together to complete projects can be some examples of how we can participate in our community to make it a better place to live for everyone.

Another great thing about helping our communities is sharing our strengths and covering each other's weaknesses! Some of us may be creative, adding artwork to the scenery. In contrast, others are great craftsmen, building structures to support businesses and homes. No matter your talent, you're sure to find ways to help!

What did I learn?

God asks us to help our communities in any way we can, as doing so helps everyone together and as a group!

Praise Through Music

Scripture: "My heart, O God is steadfast, I will sing and make music."

- Psalms 57:5

Did you know we can even praise God through music? Ever since the beginning of our gatherings, followers of God turned to songs and instruments to share excitement for how amazing God can truly be!

Although some songs are made for fun, others can be written with deep meanings of faith, hope, and overcoming big challenges. Music can be incredibly meaningful for the player and the listener, and our ways of praising God through music are no different.

Music can share God's message in a variety of ways too. From pop to rock, rap to folk, artists have a ton of ways they might make a song to share God's word and values!

The next time you listen to one of your favorite songs, think about why it became one of your favorites. Does it uplift or encourage you? Does it share a similar message even if it does not mention God? You may be surprised by what you find!

What did I learn?

God's lessons can be shared and praised through music. Sometimes even in songs not specifically about God, we can find His lessons being shared.

God's Generosity

Scripture: "God will supply every need of yours according to his riches in glory in Christ Jesus."

- Philippians 4:19

One of God's natural characteristics is His generosity and mercy. Just as He wishes for us to be generous at all times, God sets the greatest example with His own generosity!

No matter the situation, God works to act mercifully. Through His love, God hopes to reward us all for doing good. It delights Him to help us out, too, whenever we may ask!

One of the biggest ways God shows us His generosity is through forgiveness. Through Jesus's biggest sacrifice, God had decided to be generous in His forgiveness of all our wrongdoings for the past, present, and future…all we must do is work towards improvement and ask for His help!

By being generous with His mercy, God keeps us from wanting. Through faith and understanding, we are never without God's help. He will never leave us to worry nor fail us in our true wishes.

What did I learn?

God is always merciful and generous towards all that we need.

How am I Part of God's Plan?

Scripture: "Perhaps you were born for such a time as this."

- Ester 4:14

When you have big goals in mind, how do you start working on them? Most of the time, we begin the first steps of reaching our goals by planning them out. Whether for a big vacation or a small journey to our local park, planning helps ensure we have all the things we need to do, enjoy ourselves and meet our end goal!

Imagine you can tell the future. What goals do you think you would be successful in achieving? Of course, too far in the future can be hard for us to see when we try to plan things out, but fortunately, God can guide us to where we are, where we once were, and even where we need to be!

Although we might not be able to see all of it yet, God has big plans for us. He always wishes us the best, and our willingness to listen to His words will guide us toward our goals no matter what.

What did I learn?

God has big plans for everyone He has created on Earth. We cannot always see His entire plan, but with faith can follow Him to success.

Sharing our Gifts From God

Scripture: "Do not neglect to do good and to share what you have, for such sacrifices are pleasing to God."

- Hebrews 13:16

You are created completely uniquely in God's vision. Everyone is unique in many ways, and our gifts and talents are no exception!

There are many gifts and hobbies that we can find in life, and there are ways to honor God in all of them. From being good at video games, school, and sports, to have a gift for dancing, singing, or art, we must explore and find ways to grow and share our talents with others and the Lord.

No matter your gifts, they have meaning and the opportunity to serve God daily. Art of all types can be shared, bringing happiness to many. With good grades, you can help teach others. You can act as a positive role model and encourage others on a sports or gaming team! Even if you aren't sure your gifts could be helpful, it's best to have faith that God will give us the right opportunities to use them

What did I learn?

God has given us unique gifts; we should share them with the world for good!

Jealousy Beware!

Scripture: "A heart at peace gives life to the body, but envy rots the bones."

- Proverbs 14:30

God always teaches us to be grateful for all we have and are blessed with. Unfortunately, there are a lot of temptations in the world that may encourage us differently!

When we become jealous or too distracted by what others may have that we do not, it can lead to feelings of false insecurity and greed. God also mentions that if it is not taken care of properly, jealousy can grow into envy that tempts us away from His word and rules.

It can be dangerous for us to feel jealous or envious, so we should work hard to be happy for our friends and thankful for what God has helped us with. Above all, God hopes to spend time with us, listening and making sure He can keep a strong relationship with each and every one of us, and jealousy can keep us from Him. Jealousy is silly, as everybody has their own journey to follow anyway!

What did I learn?

Jealousy can be dangerous, and God hopes we do not become jealous ever, as it distracts us from what is important; following Him and cheering on our friends.

Greed No More

Scripture: "A greedy man stirs up strife, but the one who trusts in the Lord will be enriched."

- Proverbs 28:25

Just as He promises, God always ensures that we have all the things we need to stay safe and comfortable. In addition, God even gives us plenty extra that we ask for!

Being greedy means that instead of asking and being thankful for what we receive, we always ask for more than our fair share.

Pretend you see a bowl of candy at school or church with a sign that says 'take one,' sitting by itself with nobody else around. If the bowl has your favorite candy, it can be tempting to take much more than one piece! Would you still take one piece so others can have candy too?

This example is similar to what God asks of us. If we are greedy and take all the candy, or if someone took it all before we saw the bowl ourselves, it would not be fair. On the other hand, if we obey God and defy greed, everybody wins!

> **Prayer :**
>
> Dear Lord, thank you for what I have and all the blessings you have given me. Let me lean towards your word whenever I may feel tempted by greed!

What did I learn?

God wishes for us to stay away from greed or wanting too much, as He hopes for us to be generous instead.

God Protects Us

Scripture: "The Lord is faithful, and he will strengthen you and protect you from the evil one."

— Thessalonians 3:3

It is no secret that life can be dangerous. We also know that through everything, one of God's promises is that He will protect us in many ways we may not even expect yet.

A protector is somebody that works hard to keep something from harm. Some examples in our everyday lives are our family, friends, and various other grown-up leaders. Our protectors have big jobs keeping us from harm and teaching us how to eventually be protectors ourselves!

It could be scary if we did not have those who care and help to protect each other like we do, but fortunately, we also have God's protection 24/7.

God is our greatest protector from harm every second of the day. He also keeps a strong watch on our well-being, carrying our worries so that we may have peace and safety every day.

What did I learn?

God is very watchful of us and works hard every second to protect us, even giving us the help we may need through each other.

Through Good and Bad Times

Scripture: "Be still and know that I am God; I will be exalted among the nations. I will be exalted in the earth."

— Psalm 46:10

God is truly good, and He shows us this in various ways. As we go throughout our day, good and bad things can happen. We can play a new game but feel bad when we don't win a level on the first try. Win or lose, good or bad, God will be with us.

Though God is the greatest good and promises to take care of us, He also mentions we may have some challenges to work through. Our challenges can feel big or small too, but they are never impossible with God.

It brings us comfort when we realize that God is with us even in the most challenging of bad times. We know He is listening to our struggles and is encouraging us to move forward. As mentioned before, this is where we can find the silver lining in bad situations!

Overall it is normal to have good and bad experiences as we grow up, but with God's help, we can worry less since we have faith He will be with us forever.

> **Prayer :**
>
> Dear Lord, thank you for watching over me and helping me every day through both easy and hard times!

What did I learn?

God is with us and listening through good and bad times.

Learning From God's Creations

Scripture: "In his hand is the life of every creature and the breath of all mankind"

- Job 12:10

In the beginning, God had created the land, sea, and all that lived upon them. Through this, there are many creatures and beautiful landscapes from which people have taken inspiration for years and years.

As we explore all that God's world offers us, we should learn more about His creations and how they are cared for just as we are.

Many of God's animals especially have some of the same needs as we do. From the biggest ant to the largest elephant, animals look for safety, food, and community, just as we do!

No matter the season, plants change to sleep for winter, knowing it will be warm again, and animals can find what they need in the hardest of times. Even with our differences in living, God's creatures and lands are good examples of going with the flow of God's plan.

Prayer :

Dear Lord, your creations on Earth are amazing! I hope to learn from their ways, putting my trust in your promises just as they do.

What did I learn?

God's creations found in nature, animals, and even our own cities are something to celebrate, learn from, and admire!

The Greatest Sacrifice

Scripture: "He is the propitiation for our sins, and not for ours only but also for the sins of the whole world."

- John 2:2

God gives mercy in all things. One huge example of God's forgiveness and acceptance is through the sacrifice of Jesus.

God's son, Jesus, was perfect, just like His father, doing only good and working through many miracles. Among many others, Jesus had healed the sick, cured the blind, and even provided food for those in need!

As Jesus was made without sin, he preached to many how to live in the ways of God, but as some didn't like this, Jesus chose to make the greatest sacrifice.

Jesus had planned to sacrifice himself to God, so everybody's sins were forgiven, now and forever. Because of Jesus, we can now humbly ask God for forgiveness and be granted it. Overall, Jesus wanted the same goodness for us as God had, and together they allow us to be the best we can be!

What did I learn?

Jesus's sacrifice for all of humanity was a big deal to God and allowed us to seek forgiveness through His mercy.

Why do we Celebrate Easter?

Scripture: "They found the stone rolled away from the tomb, but when they entered, they did not find the body of the Lord Jesus.

- Luke 24:2

What is your favorite thing about Easter? Getting candy, seeing the Easter Bunny, and sharing a meal with family are all great events, but why do we celebrate them?

Long ago, before Easter was celebrated as we know it today, Jesus had been preaching throughout the Holy Land, sharing God's word. Of course, with this good word being spread, some were skeptical of Jesus's teachings or even angry that he was sharing the word of God.

In the end, those who disliked Jesus crucified him and eventually laid him to rest in a tomb covered by a huge boulder. Nothing could move it or get in or out of the tomb!

Finally, God decided to follow through with the last part of His plan for Jesus. After Jesus died for everyone's sins, he was resurrected and ascended to heaven again! Today, we celebrate all that Jesus had done, his rising, and a time of renewal through Easter services and celebrations!

> **Prayer :**
>
> God, thank you for allowing Jesus to provide the ultimate selfless act of carrying all our sins. Let us celebrate his return to heaven through Easter activities!

What did I learn?

Easter celebrates an important, miraculous event: the resurrection of Jesus!

God Uplifts Us

Scripture: "In the world you will have tribulation, but take heart; I have overcome the world."

- John 16:33

Whenever we are feeling down, discouraged or sad, there is always one way we can turn; toward God!

No matter how low we may feel, God is always there to listen, letting us have our burden picked up by His encouraging support. God is truly one of the best listeners that we could ever ask for. More than anything, it makes God happy to see us happy!

God is our greatest friend when sharing our thoughts and worries. While it may take a little bit of time to see God's promises grow and take place on the outside, once we speak to God about our troubles, we instantly feel relief and comfort deep in our hearts on the inside.

Above all, God works hard to remove our stormy rain clouds by turning them into rainbows and promising sunny skies ahead!

What did I learn?

Whenever we are down, God can help us find ways to lift our spirits.

God Loves our Differences!

Scripture: "For in Christ Jesus you are all sons of God, through faith."

- Galatians 3:26

One big fact of our world is that God has created each and every person differently. From our favorite foods to our gifts and talents, God appreciates our differences and makes us uniquely us!

In general, we are all alike in how we were created in God's image, but God is very creative. Using the same mold, God sculpted each of us as unique on the inside and outside.

Imagine you are in a field of flowers that all look the same. Would you be able to tell them apart? It would be very hard! Instead of keeping us all the same, God found it more interesting to give us differences. Even identical twins have a difference between them!

Just as God loves and enjoys how different we can be head to toe, we are asked to love our differences, too, especially as it makes the world a more interesting place!

What did I learn?

God has created us all differently but under the same love. Therefore, He wishes for us to love each other and our differences just as much.

God is Worldwide

Scripture: "Indeed as I live, all the earth will be filled with the glory of the Lord."

- Numbers 14:21

When Jesus spread the word of God, it was only in a small section of the Holy Land, but today, the word of God has spread across the globe!

From Europe, Asia, and Africa to the Americas, God has many followers across the land, with countless churches and congregations.

Occasionally, people even volunteer worldwide to share God's word and perform good deeds in His name.

Although it is amazing to see all the variations and ways God can influence the lives of so many across the world, the best part is that God is truly available in each and every one of those places!

Because He is up in heaven, God can be with us all at once as He watches over the entire world, listening to our prayers and praise.

> **Prayer :**
>
> Dear Lord, it is amazing how much your word can travel! I find it encouraging that no matter where I go, I can find you there with me.

What did I learn?

God will be with us no matter where we are or live in the world.

Loving God's Creatures

Scripture: "The righteous care for the needs of their animals."
- Proverbs 12:10

Do you have a favorite animal? Whether it's a big, furry bear, or a tiny house cat, God's creatures come in many shapes, sizes, and forms as they live with and around us.

From the greatest deep sea whales to the tiniest insect, God had made all creatures with a job to do on Earth we should appreciate. Even scaly, creepy animals have their purpose!

If you have a pet at home or have spent time with a friend or family member that does, you know how important it is to take care of them. Feeding, playing, and ensuring the pet has a good place to rest is a big job, but it makes God smile to see you share so much love with His creatures daily!

No matter how we share our love and kindness towards God's animals, it will truly be appreciated by both the Lord and our new critter friends as well!

What did I learn?

God's creatures are magnificent and beautiful in their own ways! We should love them just as He does.

God Keeps our Secrets

Scripture: "Would not God find this out? For He knows the secrets of the heart."

- Psalm 44:21

Have you ever been told a secret? Sometimes keeping secrets can be hard, especially if the news we are told is exciting, such as what a surprise gift will be!

Fortunately, no matter what we are speaking about, we can always rely on God to keep our secrets forever and ever. One of your closest relationships as you grow up will be with God.

From daily prayers to asking God for help in times we need it, there are countless times when we will share our thoughts and wishes with God that we may even be too nervous to tell our friends yet…especially if we're planning something big to surprise them!

Because He knows our hearts and wishes, God works hard to keep our secrets and make our dreams possible every day.

What did I learn?

We can express and share anything we need with God, as He is our confidant.

How Can We Pray?

Scripture: "Look to the Lord and his strength; seek his face always."

- Chronicles 16:11

How many ways can you think of praying? As God encourages any type of studying and speaking to Him about His word, He has allowed many different types of prayer to suit many needs.

Traditionally, many of us may wish to pray in a group setting in church. Whether in a youth class or all together for an altogether sermon, group prayer has been a key part of communities for hundreds of years.

Group prayer can be very encouraging, but there are times when we wish to speak to

God on a more private level too. For these times, we can choose to pray by ourselves.

No matter the timing of when we wish to pray, God will never be upset with us for wanting to speak with Him! He loves to speak with us at all times of the day or night, especially when we are looking for His guidance.

What did I learn?

God has given us many different ways we can pray to Him…we are always able to choose the favorite that works best for us!

Making Time for God

Scripture: "But seek first the kingdom of God and his righteousness, and all these things will be added to you."

- Matthew 6:33

Whenever we need His help, God is there for us. One way we can give back the support God always provides for our hopes, dreams, and even worries is to make time for Him every single day!

It's no secret that our lives can get busy with what we need to do each day. Things like chores, school, and hobbies can take up a big part of the day, leaving just a little bit of time left to unwind each day…and sometimes, even then, we try to fit in one last game before bed!

God loves that we have so many things we are accomplishing or having fun at, but even during the busiest of times, we should make some time in our day for God. Whether it's right before bed or on the way to an event, we can always pause to ask God for safety and guidance in all that we do.

What did I learn?

Even on the busiest of days, we should strive to make room for God in our lives no matter what.

Keep God's World Clean

Scripture: "The Lord God took the man and put him in the garden of Eden to work it and keep it."

— Genesis 2:15

There are so many ways we can show our love for God's world, and one of them is through our work to help keep it clean!

Keeping things clean can take a fair share of hard work, but it's always nice to enjoy the results of a job well done! From encouraging our family to choose earth-friendly options for our home to cleaning up our local parks and schools, keeping God's and our shared world clean can be a fun and rewarding experience.

Just as you keep your own things tidied up and cared for, God asks for us to care for our land as well. Not only is it helpful to clean up for animals and plants which can't take care of their areas themselves, but it allows us to appreciate all the beauty that God had created too.

What did I learn?

God had created our world with such wonder and beauty! He would surely love for us to help out in caring for and keeping it as clean as we can.

Showing Our Respect

Scripture: "In everything, set them an example by doing what is good. In your teaching, show integrity and seriousness."

- Titus 2:7

What do you think of when you hear of showing respect? This is a very important lesson to God; He takes respect in all forms very seriously!

Overall, respect means that we take action in all that we do by considering or thinking of how others would feel. Respecting another person's ideas means that we understand that they can make their own choices, and we will accept them and value them as they are.

Often, you may hear the words 'respect your elders,' which adds an important lesson to God's teachings of respect…the idea that if we take the time to understand and listen to those who are older than us, they may have some great lessons to share!

Finally, along with showing respect towards each other, we should show our greatest respect towards God. After all, He respects us and our individuality each and every day!

Prayer :

Dear Lord, please help me continue to give respect to everything and everyone you wish me to. By doing so, I hope to always walk with your teachings!

What did I learn?

We should show respect in all that we do towards God and each other.

God is in All Things

Scripture: "The eyes of the Lord are in every place, keeping watch on the evil and the good."

- Proverbs 15:3

From the biggest events happening worldwide to the smallest ones, God can be found in all things. God is very busy but always finds time for all of us, no matter what!

It is no surprise that we tend to get very busy. Still, with all the responsibilities God can have, it may sound surprising to hear how much God can be involved with us.

No matter where we are or what we do, if we stop for a minute and take the time to listen or to look closely at our surroundings, we can find God's hand at work.

From beautiful creations found in nature to the little miracles that can happen throughout the day. In these, God keeps watch on us and protects us, and works little by little to care for our lives, even when we don't know it!

What did I learn?

If you look closely, you can find God in many parts of your life!

Trust in God

Scripture: "Blessed is the man who trusts in the Lord, whose trust is the Lord'

- Jeremiah 17:7

When we walk with God, we learn to trust God. Your trust in God's plans and ways is very important; without it, He couldn't be successful in your life!

God proves time and time again just how much He cares for us. Through acts of graciousness and forgiveness, to acting as a guide in directing us on our next step, God often asks for our trust in His plans.

Although it would make some things easier, we don't have the power to tell the future, unfortunately, so we must often rely on our faith and trust in God. God cannot always show us how things will be ok, but we can always take His promise for it!

Above all, our trust in God lets God put His trust in us too. At all times, rain or shine, we can truly depend on God and His plans. After all, God never breaks our trust or any promises He may make.

What did I learn?

God is faithful and dedicated, so we can put all of our trust in Him.

Patience Takes Practice

Scripture: "Better to be patient than a warrior, and better to have self-control than to capture a city."

- Proverbs 16:32

Think of the last time you really, really wanted something. Maybe it was a new toy or a cool game on your birthday wishlist. It could also be a fun trip on your bucket list, such as going to an amusement park or watching a brand-new movie in theaters.

We often have to have the patience to wait for our rewards or gifts, and for God, we may also need to wait to receive His blessings.

Sometimes, patience can be hard to practice. Other times it can be really easy as time seems to fly by, but no matter what we're patient for, we always know it's worth it, especially with God's gifts!

No matter if it's a long or short waiting time, we should not fear that God will always be in control. He listens to us and understands what we want and need. Still, occasionally he will ask us to practice our patience in receiving His blessings.

What did I learn?

God blesses us every day and truly listens to our prayers, but sometimes we must be patient to see the results!

Listen Carefully

Scripture: "Listen to advice and accept instruction, and in the end you will be wise."

- Proverbs 19:20

When we are seeking answers to new things or asking questions about something we don't know, what can we do to learn our best? In these and all times when we are looking for guidance, God will surely show us the way if we listen carefully!

There are many times when God asks us to listen carefully. For example, our parents or teachers might be working hard to show us the best way to complete a task or how to be safe.

In all things that we are listening to, we must listen and be willing to accept instructions on how to do better, especially when it comes to God's word! No matter the lesson, as long as we keep our ears and hearts open, God can always lead us the right way through our listening skills.

What did I learn?

God asks us to listen carefully in all that we do…this way, you can best understand His guidance!

Be Charitable

Scripture: "Each one must give as he has decided in his heart, not reluctantly or under compulsion, for God loves a cheerful giver."

- Corinthians 9:7

Have you heard of the saying, 'it's better to give than to receive? If so, you already understand part of why God believes being charitable is so important!

No matter the situation, being charitable and helping each other in any way we can is a great idea. When we help each other out, it makes God happy, too, as we share His hopes to spread peace and happiness.

God works hard to give us plenty, but He also gives us chances to find ways to be charitable and share our blessings and possibly His guidelines too!

Being charitable can come from anywhere, from volunteering your time to help out somebody else to sharing something essential that you have extra. No matter the cause, God will surely give us the right time and ability to be charitable in many more ways than we could possibly imagine!

What did I learn?

It makes God happy when we can be charitable towards one another, and He will show us the way to get started too!

Get Active With God

Scripture: "Glory in his holy name; let the hearts of those who seek the Lord rejoice! Seek the Lord and his strength; seek his presence continually! "

- Chronicles 16:10

You know it's important to take care of your body with proper exercise, but do you know you should also be active in another way?

Of course, regular exercise is essential to growing healthy and strong, but we must also be active spiritually with God. From praying regularly to reading scripture and even sharing his values in our daily life, there are many ways to stay active in spirit.

No matter where we are or what we're doing, there is always time to pause and reflect on God's word. This can be as easy as regularly asking what the Lord would like to teach us daily!

Keeping active with God and His word is truly rewarding in many ways. No matter how often we seek Him, He will be with us!

What did I learn?

God wishes for us to have a healthy body and spirit as we seek his guidance.

Eating Healthy, God's Way

Scripture: "So whether you eat or drink or whatever you do, do it all for the glory of God."

- 1 Corinthians 10:31

Candy and snacks are tons of fun, but it's also important to have a healthy diet. As we were all created years ago, God ensured that we had all the nutrients and supplies we needed. He always hopes for the best for us, especially when it comes to our health!

From fruits and vegetables to high protein snacks such as nuts, meats, and even dairy, No matter what we eat, it's incredibly important for us to make sure our diet Is balanced with healthy foods and our favorite snacks.

God has made many different types of food for us to try, so the options are limitless. Above all, it's not bad to treat yourself from time to time, but God wants to ensure we can still do our best work by ensuring our energy is balanced by the fuel we give it.

Prayer :

Dear Lord, thank you for my health and ability to keep my body healthy.

What did I learn?

God takes our health and nutrition seriously and wishes us to keep a balanced diet!

Be Like a Duck

Scripture: "For if you forgive other people when they sin against you, your heavenly Father will also forgive you."

- Matthew 6:14

Have you ever had an experience where someone was mean to you? What did you think to do in response?

Sometimes we may face the challenge of dealing with mean people or rude thoughts even if we didn't do anything to deserve it.

With God's help, we can be strong and not have these situations bother us! For example, if you look closely at a duck's feathers while swimming, you can see tiny beads of water rolling down its sides; the water simply rolls off the duck's back!

When it comes to mean words, God asks us to forgive and be like a duck…by letting the negativity not bother us and, in turn, share only kindness and forgiveness, no matter how hard it can be.

What did I learn?

We should always forgive and work hard to thwart negativity…when in doubt, be like a duck!

Helping Hands

Scripture: "Each of you should give what you have decided in your heart to give, not reluctantly or under compulsion, for God loves a cheerful giver."

- Corinthians 10:31

Imagine you were at home relaxing and playing games, but you see one of your family members working hard to get chores done. What would you do?

In all situations, God hopes we will always offer a helping hand if we can. Just as we wouldn't want to work hard on our own, we should always help others if we have the time!

Whether it's helping out with chores, assisting in the classroom, or even something as short and simple as helping a friend make a decision, every time we reach out and help, it makes God incredibly happy.

Finally, we can find it incredibly rewarding to lend a helping hand. Doing good makes us feel good in our hearts and even spreads positivity toward those we are helping.

What did I learn?

God loves it when we lend a helping hand to our friends…and it makes everyone involved feel good too!

Never Give Up!

Scripture: "I have fought the good fight, I have finished the race, I have kept the faith."

- Timothy 4:7

Think of a movie you have seen where the good guys have to save the world. It's definitely not an easy task and takes a lot of time. It may seem easier to give up and go home along the way, but what would happen if they did just that?

Just like the heroes or good guys in movies, sometimes God will give us challenges that we think we might not be able to complete. It may seem really easy to give up too, but He knows that if you keep at it, you'll be able to be successful. In all things, God hopes we never give up!

To never give up means to persevere. To persevere means to keep trying, no matter how hard it might seem, because in the end, you never truly know when you will succeed until you have kept trying!

We should always have faith that God will set us up for success in anything that we set our hearts to, and we should never take giving up lightly!

Prayer :

Dear Lord, thank you for being with me and especially through all of the challenges I may see. I hope to keep my faith in you and persevere through it all.

What did I learn?

God may create challenges in our lives, but He knows we are able to persevere and go past them.

Represent God's Values

Scripture: "Whoever claims to live in him must walk as Jesus did."

- John 2:6

God often takes time to share His values and requests with us, but what does He want us to do with this knowledge?

No matter what we do or where we go, God asks us to work hard to live with the same values as He does. From making sure we are honest and trustworthy to others to even being sincere in our asking for forgiveness for our mistakes, God hopes for us to always be the very best, we can be!

God understands that as people here on earth, we are bound to make mistakes. We aren't perfect, and that's ok, but when mistakes are made, God always gives us a chance to learn from them and do even better next time!

Just like Jesus and many other followers of God before us, we should continue our mission to follow His values as best as we can since it can not only encourage us to keep our relationship with God close but can influence others to do the same!

What did I learn?

God has created many specific values He follows and would like us to follow.

What Does the Cross Stand For?

Scripture: "He himself bore our sins in his body on the cross, so that we might die to sins and live for righteousness; by his wounds you have been healed."

- Peter 2:24

From Christmas displays to church pews and wall decorations to fine jewelry, the cross can be seen in many different places or settings, but what exactly does it stand for?

The cross or crucifix is one of the most important and recognizable symbols of God and His followers. A symbol can be used to show the meaning or importance of a subject without the need for words, and the cross is no exception.

In general, the cross is an example of faith. In one of the most important parts of the bible, Jesus was crucified on a cross and then resurrected, showing a great example of how God had given life to Jesus again through his sacrifice. Through this, the cross had turned from a horrible fate to a symbol of faith, hope, and God's love for us.

What did I learn?

For God, the cross is a special symbol, representing hope, faith, and, most importantly, His love for us all!

A Christmas Miracle!

Scripture: "Therefore the Lord himself will give you a sign: The virgin will conceive and give birth to a son, and will call him Immanuel." - Isaiah 7:14

Christmas is one of the biggest holidays in the world, but do you know of God's most important story that has inspired our Christmas celebrations?

Long ago, God told us that Mary and Joseph had been traveling far and wide, as the miracle of baby Jesus's birth was about to come true! Jesus had been born in a humble shelter, but all the angels and people soon realized he would be the King of Kings!

In the time before Jesus, plenty of people were lost from God's word, and Jesus would eventually grow to teach and heal everyone that praised the Lord.

From his beginnings in birth to his resurrection and eventual return to God, Jesus had many tasks ahead of him to ensure everybody's sins were redeemed through God's mercy.

> **Prayer :**
>
> Dear Lord, thank you for giving us the best miracle we could have in the birth of Jesus! Please help me to always reflect on the importance of why we celebrate Christmas.

What did I learn?

Christmas is one of the most important holidays to celebrate…it represents the miracle of baby Jesus being born!

Exercise for a Healthy Spirit

Scripture: "Do you not know that your bodies are temples of the Holy Spirit, who is in you, whom you have received from God?"

- Corinthians 6:19

To keep our bodies healthy and happy, there's one thing that we can always do; exercise!

God teaches us in many ways that our body is a temple of the Holy Spirit, meaning that we should take the very best care of it. From making sure we're taking care of ourselves the best we can through our food and nutrition to our daily exercise habits, there are many ways we can make sure we stay strong and balanced.

Of course, God doesn't expect us to all look the same or exercise too much, but to respect our bodies and give it what it needs just as we respect His teachings.

God has given us many ways to exercise that can be fun, too, from hiking, swimming, and biking, to just playing sports outside with friends. No matter what we choose, it's easy to find activities that work for everyone!

What did I learn?

God made us so we could do many things! In all that we do, we should work to keep ourselves physically safe and healthy through exercise and good food.

Praying for Others

Scripture: "And pray in the Spirit on all occasions with all kinds of prayers and requests."

- Ephesians 6:18

We all have our own responsibilities, but what should you do when you see somebody struggling with a challenge of their own?

Many times, God asks us to help out and lend a hand to others, but there can be other times when you aren't able to solve a friend's problem by yourself. But there's no need to fear. Prayer will still be here for us!

Just as when we have faced hard times, God encourages us to pray for others. Some problems are really big, and we might not know every little part of it like God does, but through prayer, we can share our encouragement with our friends and help lift their spirits.

God listens to all prayers and requests for help, and your genuine support, both in actions and prayer, can be just as reassuring to those in need!

> **Prayer :**
>
> Dear Lord, thank you for being the great listener that you are. Just as you hear my prayers, I know you hear my friends too. In this, let me help as best as I can by praying for others in what they need from you.

What did I learn?

When we notice others struggling in their life, God hopes we will not only reach out if we can help but to pray for their well-being.

Healthy Mind, Healthy Body

Scripture: "A happy heart makes the face cheerful, but heartache crushes the spirit."

- Proverbs 15:13

Exercising ourselves physically through sports, playing games, and hobbies are important, but what about our mind and mental health?

Just as God encourages us to exercise and take care of our bodies physically as a temple, He also means to encourage us to take care of how we think or our inner bodies.

Negative thoughts of anxiety, sadness, or even anger can really bring us down and keep us from doing our best for God. No matter what you are worried or upset about, don't forget you can rely on God to keep your mind healthy!

God understands our minds can be bothered by responsibilities in life but wishes for us to take time for ourselves to reset, speak with God, and rest so we can keep going in confidence, happy, and healthy!

Prayer :

Dear Lord, thank you for watching over me in all that I do and encouraging my good health in both mind, body, and spirit. May I always lean on you to ease my thoughts and stay balanced!

What did I learn?

God finds it very important for us to take care of ourselves not just physically but mentally as well!

Stand Up for Others

Scripture: "We who are powerful need to be patient with the weakness of those who don't have power, and not please ourselves."

- Romans 15:1

In the Bible, God's followers have seen many enemies and bullies that they must encounter on their own journeys. Just as this happened a long time ago, you may also have to face your own bullies!

No matter what, God encourages us to be kind even if others aren't. Of course, some people do not follow this rule and choose to pick on, be rude, or just plain make fun of others instead.

In these situations, God encourages us to stand up for those who are being singled out! Whether it's being a good samaritan yourself by offering a helping hand or friendship to the person being hurt or even telling a grownup of the situation, there are many ways we can stand up for and support others.

What did I learn?

God asks us to be strong and stand up to bullies that are being mean to others… kindness is always best!

Love is Kind

Scripture: "Love is patient, love is kind, it isn't jealous, it doesn't brag, it isn't arrogant."

- Corinthians 13:4

Think of all the places and times you have experienced true love. God's true love can come in many different ways, and it isn't exactly the same true love from fairytales!

Often, people think of love when they are grown-up and looking for God to guide them in getting married, but love can be shown in Plenty of other ways too.

From parents and family, friends, and even with our four-legged, furry friends, God shows us that no matter how love is created in our lives, it is through kindness, patience, and selflessness. You probably show your love towards others in this way too!

No matter the situation, God helps us to always show our love through kindness, just as we receive love in that way! From taking action to show how we care to just listening to each other openly, God will surely help guide us in all our good relationships!

What did I learn?

God's love can be shown in many ways through friends and family. No matter what, it will be true, kind, and will never let you down.

Goodbye Anxiety!

Scripture: "Don't be anxious about anything; rather, bring up all of your requests to God in your prayers and petitions, along with giving thanks."

- Philippians 4:6

Whenever you start to feel really worried, what do you do? We are incredibly fortunate that on both our good and bad days, God will always listen to us to help us say goodbye to our anxieties!

Most of the time, our anxieties can come from not knowing what is next in our lives, but God can always reassure us that He will be with us. By talking to friends, family, and counselors, we can feel better and learn more about why we are concerned, but God plays an important part in doing this too.

He helps us out, especially during those times when we feel like we are unsure of who to talk to also. Just like a school counselor can help you out when you are struggling with your grades, God can help in the toughest parts of life!

What did I learn?

God doesn't want us to feel anxious or worried about anything we must do. Instead, He asks to help us with all our worries!

Endings Aren't All Bad

Scripture: "The end of something is better than its beginning."

- Ecclesiastes 7:8

God made our world with a lot of Change. From the season's around us to our own time growing up and learning new things, sometimes changes can bring endings and new beginnings.

Mentioning the end of something can come with a bad rap, but God reminds us that there is always good to be found, even in endings! The end of something like a school year, moving to a new place, or even something small like the end of watching our favorite movie or show can bring a lot of emotions.

From sadness to worry, hope to excitement, we don't always know what our next journey will take us on. Still, we should rest assured that God is with us every step to ensure we are always following His plans for us every step of the way.

What did I learn?

God is always in the know about what comes next in our lives. Sometimes when something ends, it's actually the start of another good or better beginning than the last!

God Will Return!

Scripture: "Therefore, stay alert! You don't know what day the Lord is coming."

- Matthew 24:42

A long time ago, people like Jesus and Moses had spoken to God, listening to His word as guidance. Jesus was a big helper in this, too, as he shared God's word all over, bringing forgiveness to us all.

Today, God and Jesus are both busy at work in heaven, so we can't see them physically with us here on earth and have to use our prayers and studies to learn and speak for now.

Even so, God promises that we will return to Him one day! When our time is over on earth, and we have learned all we should, we will finally meet God and go through His judgment to enter heaven.

It may be a long way away, but you can be reassured that God will return to see you again in person, just as when you were created!

What did I learn?

When the time is right, God will return to us and bless everyone who has followed him.

Anything is Possible With God

Scripture: " I can do all this through him who gives me strength."

- Philippians 4:13

As we grow up and learn new things, we will have many challenges to succeed in! From playing games with friends to more serious activities like studying hard for good grades, God gives us the strength to do anything we set our minds to.

God can give us strength in many ways. In the Bible, we learn of all the miracles God and Jesus can do for everyone. From guiding them to safety to healing and providing all

His people's needs. Finally, God gives us the strength to do what we think is impossible. Looking closely, we can see His miracles working in our daily lives!

God always cares for us and helps us with our needs. Through His guidance, we can always figure out the best thing to do in any situation. With this, it can be easy to see how God gives us strength in both our minds and abilities!

What did I learn?

God does many things. He gives us strength and performs miracles, so even the impossible is possible!

God Gives You Rest

Have you ever had a long, busy day of school or chores? Life can be busy, but God understands this and helps us take the time we need to rest.

From homework to after-school sports, clubs, and even shopping trips or fun days out, we might have plenty of fun things to do and responsibilities with our families. It feels good to get our to-do lists done, but breaks are important too.

With this, God also works to take care of us and help add balance back to our lives.

Today, many families take a break to focus on God on Sundays. From going to church or even studying God's word and resting at home, this is just one way we can look to God to help us rest and renew for more busy days to come.

No matter how you look to God for guidance when you are most tired, He will help give you rest, lifting both physical and spiritual burdens.

What did I learn?

God understands that life can make you really tired sometimes. Through Him, he helps you rest from all the hustle and bustle of your responsibilities anytime!

Be Honest

Scripture: "Do not lie to each other, since you have taken off your old self with its practices."
- Colossians 3:9

God always goes by the rule that 'Honesty is the best policy,' but have you ever experienced a difficult situation where it might be hard, to be honest? Even in harder times, we must always be honest and truthful!

Imagine you broke your parents' favorite mug by accident. What would you think to do? Even when we make mistakes, such as accidentally breaking something, it is always better, to be honest with those we care about and ourselves to fix it.

Being honest in every situation we may find ourselves in is very important to God, as He will always ask us to stay with the truth.

Sometimes we may feel pressured to tell even a little lie, but no matter what, even small lies can cause big trouble!

What did I learn?

God is honest in all He does and wishes for us to be honest too!

God Lifts Our Sadness

Scripture: "The Lord is close to the brokenhearted, and saves those who are crushed in spirit."

- Psalm 34:18

It's no secret that God is great in all that he helped us with but did you know that he even helps lift our sadness in the worst of times?

Naturally, things in life can bring us down and make us sad or discouraged, but especially in these times, we should remember that God is with us. When we pray to God, just as we can ask Him for guidance in what we should do next or talk about our worries, we can also ask Him to help relieve our feelings of sadness.

God can uplift our spirits in many ways, from helping our day become just a little brighter to showing us the positives and hope that the future will improve. God promises that even the saddest or scariest of times are only temporary and will pass. No matter what, God is on our side forever and always, through the good and the bad times.

What did I learn?

Whenever we are down or sad, God is always there to help brighten our day and make us feel better.

It's Not About The Money

Scripture: "Keep your life free from love of money, and be content with what you have, for he has said, "I will never leave you nor forsake you."

- Hebrews 13:5

Lots of things in our world involve using money, but what does God think of it?

As a rule of thumb, money is used for fun, shelter, and even food. Acting as a resource to trade goods and services, but just like any other thing in life, too much of it can lead to bad consequences if you aren't careful.

Many objects or things in our life, like money, are temporary. We have our turn with money to use for what we need, but we should not let it be the most important thing in our life as we get older!

God encourages us to keep important things at the top of our priority list. Our relationship with Him and those we love are much more important and long-lasting than any object in life!

What did I learn?

Money may be used for many things in our lives, but God does not want it to be the most important thing for us…He should always be put first!

Reunited Again

Scripture: "Therefore you too have grief now; but I will see you again, and your heart will rejoice, and no one will take your joy away from you."

- John 16:22

When we lose a loved one, we can deeply feel sad and miss them. Fortunately, even in these times, God is with us, supporting us all along the way.

Just as God understands our daily needs in times of happiness, He is also with us through our most challenging times. Losing one that we love or anybody who positively influences our lives can be difficult to process, no matter the details.

Finally, God reminds us of positive memories to be comforted by, as well as His greatest promise of all; that we will be reunited with our loved ones again someday.

What did I learn?

When we have lost a loved one, it can be very sad and make us miss them. Fortunately, you can always be assured that they are never alone and with God until it is time to meet again.

Keep it Clean

Scripture: "Who can say, "I have kept my heart pure; I am clean and without sin"?

- Proverbs 20:9

When was the last time you cleaned your room? Don't forget to be honest!

Our parents often remind us to keep our things clean, and while it can be tough to get started, there's a very good reason for doing so!

God talks about keeping things clean differently, too, such as His goals for us to stay free of sin. From the baptisms, Jesus had invited us to perform for others, to God's guidance in staying away from things that can 'dirty' our spirits, such as stealing, lying, and hurting others, God hopes for us to keep ourselves 'clean' in the sense that we are always walking in His light.

Just as we're asked to keep our rooms or homes clean, by doing so, we can find things better and even improve how we feel about our surroundings. Staying clean by God's standards through asking for forgiveness and working hard to avoid disobeying Him helps us follow His plans even more!

> **Prayer :**
>
> Dear Lord, it might be tricky keeping my things clean at home sometimes, but with your help, I can always stay clean and pure of heart to follow your wishes!

What did I learn?

Keeping things clean helps to keep away germs and even represents God's wishes for us to stay free from sin!

Mind Your Words!

Scripture: "We demolish arguments and every pretension that sets itself up against the knowledge of God, and we take captive every thought to make it obedient to Christ."

- Corinthians 10:5

Through our studies of the Bible, we learn of all the many ways we can do good through our actions for God's wishes. Just as he tells us what we should do, God can also help us understand what is best to say too!

Overall, God teaches us to be loyal, honest, and hard-working to follow His wishes of goodness and blessings. We can also always ask God for help figuring out what to say.

God shows us that we can show our kindness and knowledge of His word through our actions and how we speak to others. Being harsh or rude to others, even when frustrated, is never a good thing to do, and it ends up making everybody feel down!

What did I learn?

Just as we should do good with our actions, God asks us to be careful with our words because they can be just as important.

Time for Rest

We work hard with God every day. We may be planning vacations and activities instead when we're not in school!

No matter how busy we are, God is always with us. Being busy is good, and we can accomplish many things through Him, but did you know resting is just as important?

When God created our world, He worked hard for days, finally leaving the seventh to rest. Just like God, we might choose our day of rest to relax and prepare for what's next.

Finally, when we are not physically resting, God shows us that we can seek rest through

Him whenever we need it. We can rest our minds and body by spending time with God!

What did I learn?

There is a time to work hard and time to rest. God encourages a healthy balance of both!

Lean on God

Scripture: "For I, the Lord your God, hold your right hand; it is I who say to you, 'Fear not, I am the one who helps you."

- Isaiah 41:13

You can lean on God to help out with any of your doubts and troubles! God gives us all the help we need to face our fears and succeed in anything we work to accomplish!

God is one of your very best friends. He understands everything you want to share with Him, and as a plus that only He can do, he even blesses you with so many good things.

Whenever times get tough, God's presence can help us in many ways through encouragement and support. He teaches us that no matter the challenge, the impossible in our lives can become possible!

In anything we might need help with, we should always seek to lean on God. He is with us and helps us overcome anything we could ever need to get through.

> **Prayer :**
>
> Dear God, no matter my challenges, I know I can always lean on you! You always bring me strength and comfort... I'm thankful I can rely on your word.

What did I learn?

No matter what we are working through, you can rest easy knowing you can rely on God in many ways!

What is Love?

Scripture: "Let all that you do be done in love."

- Corinthians 16:4

It is no secret that God shows us how much He loves us very often! God encourages us to be strong, helps us when we are down, and so much more.

With God, we can cast all worries aside. He truly loves us just as much as we love Him. No matter the consequences or where we go, God makes big promises to fulfill the needs in our lives and hearts. He is always faithful to His promises too!

Jesus had worked in love too. From curing others and leading them to salvation to even showing his love through God's mercy with his greatest sacrifice, Jesus showed how much God loves us through his actions and words!

Just like God and Jesus, we should work hard to do everything in love. We can learn to make bad situations better by loving each other and looking forward to God helping solve our problems, no matter how big or small.

What did I learn?

God's love is outstanding and strong. With Him on our side, we have nothing to fear!

Practice, Practice, Practice!

Scripture: "Whatever you have learned or received or heard from me, or seen in me—put it into practice. And the God of peace will be with you."

- Philippians 4:9

Imagine you and a friend are about to play a new board game. Your friend has played before and knows all the rules and tricks to win, but you don't yet. What should you do?

Learning the rules of something new can be confusing, but with God's encouragement, we know that you can always practice and do your best. Over time you may be amazed at what you have learned to do!

Practicing means being active in what you're learning. We can practice being better at games, but we can also practice getting better at listening to God or sharing His word too!

Just as we learn the rules of that new game your friend is so good at, we should listen to God's lessons. Over time what was once confusing will make sense. Eventually, you may find yourself explaining the rules (or His word) to others all by yourself!

> **Prayer :**
>
> Dear God, through your patience, I am confident that I can practice and learn all that you ask me to! I hope to always practice understanding your word, getting better every time!

What did I learn?

God understands we are not made to be perfect, but He did give us the ability to practice and always do better!

Study Your Best

Scripture: "He gives strength to the weary and increases the power of the weak"

- Isaiah 40:29

God encourages us to practice in everything we do, but what about schoolwork?

You probably know your favorite school subject but think of your least favorite. Is it hard to do? Does it take a long time? There's no doubt that sometimes when we are practicing to improve something, challenging subjects might feel boring to us.

Even if the subject is hard to understand, we can do plenty of things to improve our studying! From instructional videos to classroom games, God encourages us to study our best with what works best for both regular schoolwork and our bible studies. No matter what, we should never give up… God has our back in learning even the most challenging ideas!

What did I learn?

From Bible studies to schoolwork, studying can sound boring, but it is key to doing well in all that we do!

Who is Noah?

Scripture: "The LORD then said to Noah, 'Go into the ark, you and your whole family, because I have found you righteous in this generation.'"

- Genesis 7:1

One of the most iconic tales in the Bible is that of Noah and his ark, but who exactly was Noah, and what did he do?

Long ago, God noticed a lot of corruption and sin in our world, so much so that it was overwhelming all that was good! Fortunately, God found one faithful person in Noah that could lead his family and all the creatures in the area to safety while God got rid of all the danger.

With this, God told Noah to build a huge ark for all the animals to live on. This was because God created a Great Flood to cleanse the earth for over a year!

Since Noah listened to God, he was able to make sure his family and his animals were eventually able to start over again in a clean world, and God promised to never send another flood again.

What did I learn?

Noah had a big task from God…to build an ark big and strong enough to keep all animals safe from the Great Flood!

Don't Take What's Not Yours

Honesty is very important to God in all that we do. You should always stick with the truth, from your words to your actions! Just as we might be tempted to lie to others, God warns us of another way we would be dishonest.

Not being honest in what is yours is called stealing. No matter the circumstance, God wishes for us to never steal or take anything that isn't ours. If we choose to steal from others, not only does it take something away from them that they might truly need, but it makes it unfair for everybody involved. If somebody stole from you, how would you feel?

God expects us to work hard and honestly in everything we do, including staying honest with each other. The temptation to take what isn't ours can have big consequences that we can't see yet. We should rest easy understanding that with God's way and guidance, He will make sure we have anything we might need…we just have to ask!

What did I learn?

Stealing is never right in God's eyes. No matter what, you should never take what's not yours!

What is Church For?

Scripture: "For where two or three are gathered in my name, there am I among them."

- Matthew 18:20

Do you ever wonder what church is made for? Today there are many different types of churches that all work hard to worship God in their own ways, but is there anything they have in common?

No matter the name or distinction a church might have, they all serve one purpose being a house to worship and love God through creating a community. We go to church to meet like-minded friends and to study or learn about God's word!

Some churches may have different traditions, but they all serve the same purpose in hoping to do good through sharing the word of God's word and working in our communities to make them better. Many even have study groups, classrooms, and summer school programs!

What did I learn?

There are thousands of churches around today that can be very different from one another, but they all are made as a place to worship God with others.

God's Many Miracles

There is no doubt that God is a miracle worker! In what ways have you noticed His miracles working in your life?

When faced with a really hard problem, it can be hard to figure out a solution, no matter how much you think! You may even feel overwhelmed about what to expect for the future, saying that it must be impossible to work through it.

Fortunately, we can always turn to God and ask for His help! Through God, we must always remember that we can do all things. God is all-powerful and can find a solution for even the most puzzling problems through his miracles.

What did I learn?

God is all-powerful and able to create many miracles that no human could do!

How Can We Help God?

Scripture: "I lift up my eyes to the mountains— where does my help come from? My help comes from the Lord, the Maker of heaven and earth."

- Psalm 121:1

There's no doubt that God works nonstop to help us out, no matter what. He's a hard worker, all that needs to be taken care of, but what can we do to help God? Fortunately, He tells us exactly what He expects!

God is very clear on how we can help Him, no matter how big or small we are. By following God's word and lessons, He promises that we will all have the opportunity to do good to each other through His values.

Finally, God has created us with talents and abilities that can help! Through these talents, we can always find unique ways to help out God in whatever way He asks of us.

What did I learn?

One of the best ways we could help God is by listening to and following His word. This way, we can share His vision of goodness in our world!

Speak Up!

Scripture: "Speak up and judge fairly; defend the rights of the poor and needy."

- Proverbs 31:9

Picture your favorite movie or real-life hero. What makes them strong? Is it their special ability, how well they are known, or something else? In other words, what makes them a hero? Those we look up to, whether they are real or pretend, have one thing in common; they speak up for others!

Whenever we are able, God wishes for us to speak up for those who might not be able to talk for themselves. From people being bullied to times when our friends are shy, we can always offer to help them by speaking up for what they need!

Overall, God wishes for us to take care of each other in action and in our voices, defending whoever we can and asking for help from others at times because that makes us strong too!

What did I learn?

Sometimes God may ask us to be brave. He can give us the strength to speak up against anything!

Share God's Peace

Scripture: "Strive for full restoration, encourage one another, be of one mind, live in peace. And the God of love and peace will be with you."

- Corinthians 13:11

Here's a lesson to practice at home! Line up some books, dominos, or something similar in shape. Now push one over to see what happens! If they're all close to each other, a chain reaction happens, and they all can fall down.

God helps us a lot through both good and bad moods, and just like the chain reaction you made, our mood and who we share it with can cause a chain reaction too.

Even in our bad moods, we should work hard to find solutions to our problems with God's help and share His peace and love in a chain reaction instead of hurtful things to others!

Prayer :

Dear God, wherever I go, please help me share your peace and encouragement every day! You are truly a positive force of good, and I hope to always share those same feelings with all who I meet and talk to.

What did I learn?

God's biggest hope for our world is to ensure it is peaceful. We can help by bringing peace to each other every day.

God's Many Plans for Us

Scripture: "In his heart a man plans his course, but the LORD determines his steps."

- Proverbs 16:9

Plans are made in our lives each and every day. We have our morning routines, afternoon schoolwork, and weekend fun with friends all the time! But did you know God plans a lot for us that we don't see?

Even with our plans, God sometimes has His own plans for us! God listens to our big ideas and can help make them a reality through His planning.

From before you were born to many years in the future, God will work hard to plan each and every part of your life. From challenges to blessings, He will help you do exactly what you need to do no matter what!

What did I learn?

God has created each of us uniquely and has great plans for us all!

Looking For God's Work

Scripture: "God did this so that they would seek him and perhaps reach out for him and find him, though he is not far from any one of us."

— Acts 17:27

From the tiniest ants on the ground to every bird flying through the sky, and even our own busy lives, our world can be very busy!

Even in the busiest of times, when we look closely, we can see God's work in everything around us. Today, God often prefers to work under the radar and in the background.

God is always here to help us, but His work involves watching how we act, even when nobody is watching us. With this, God can always judge us fairly and make sure that we follow His word no matter what.

Like a secret spy, God still sees and helps us with everything, but He often wishes for us to seek Him instead of the other way around!

> **Prayer :**
>
> Dear God, please help me to slow down from the business of life to focus on all the blessings that you provide me. I know your work is everywhere once I look closely!

What did I learn?

God's work and blessings can be seen in everything, even if we must pay close attention to see it.

Stay Resilient

Scripture: "So do not fear, for I am with you; do not be dismayed, for I am your God. I will strengthen you and help you; I will uphold you with my righteous right hand."

- Isaiah 41:10

When we build houses, roads, and bridges, we work hard to make them last and be resilient throughout all conditions. Just as we make these objects strong, God has made us even stronger!

No matter our struggles or worries, God promises to take care of us and give us the strength we need. Even more, than the strongest bridges that have seen dozens of storms, the resilience we are given by God is worth more than we could count.

We often don't even know how strong we can be until we look back and see all we have done with God's help! Through Him, we find our resilience to weather many storms and troubles, leaving them behind us for a brighter future.

What did I learn?

God wishes for us to stay strong and endure all our struggles. With Him, this is always possible!

God Loves You

Scripture: "Keep yourselves in God's love as you wait for the mercy of our Lord Jesus Christ to bring you to eternal life."

- Jude 1:21

Not only is God our biggest advocate and helper, but He truly shines in His love for us!

God's love is unconditional. As our creator, God knows everything about us, good and bad. He praises the good and blesses us, yet he also understands that He must have us experience challenges and tests that may distract us. We aren't perfect and can make mistakes too.

God realizes this and everything, but He also notices our efforts. Instead of turning away from God, we ask for forgiveness and work hard to do better! With God's love, anything is possible. As he accepts our apologies, He reminds us that even when we weren't paying attention, He was right there supporting us!

What did I learn?

God loves us unconditionally for who we are and blesses us when we love Him back.

Don't be Disappointed

Scripture: "Do not let your hearts be troubled. You believe in God, believe also in me. My Father's house has many rooms; if that were not so, would I have told you that I am going there to prepare a place for you?"

- John 14:1

Think of the last time you got your hopes up when expecting something. We wait for many things, from new toys, games, and movie releases, to more everyday activities like waiting for a doctor's appointment.

Unfortunately, waiting can bring along disappointments when we receive something we do not expect. We may be excited about the latest action movie but unhappy with the ending.

God is unique when it comes to being disappointed. Unlike these otherworldly events, He will never disappoint. Remember, God keeps all his promises, even if we have to wait for the right time to see His blessings!

What did I learn?

Sometimes we may feel disappointed or as if God is not listening to our prayers, but we shouldn't because God will never let us down in the end.

Always Listen to God!

Scripture: "And he said to them, 'Pay attention to what you hear: with the measure you use, it will be measured to you, and still more will be added to you."

- Mark 4:24

The next time you're on a trip, ask a grown-up if you can check out the directions on a map or GPS. If you do, you may notice that you'll have to listen to instructions to reach your destination.

When we're on a big real-life journey into our next adventure, we often have to listen to God's directions! In these times, it's really important because if we don't, we could risk getting lost, just like when we follow a GPS.

 No matter the next turn we might take, God's guidance and word act as a GPS for us to safely follow. He always wants us to arrive at our destination safely, so we should always listen to His directions!

What did I learn?

We should always listen to God's word, guidance, and wishes.

God Knows Best

Scripture: "Do not conform to the pattern of this world, but be transformed by the renewing of your mind. Then you will be able to test and approve what God's will is—his good, pleasing and perfect will."

- Romans 12:2

When you're an expert on something, it makes sense that you know best about your topic, and it's no different with God!

There are a ton of things we can learn about as we keep growing up, but we might not know God has experienced it many times before.

Whenever you have a problem or are unsure of the answer to something big, don't be afraid to ask God for answers since He knows best about what we can do! Through His guidance, we can be given the answers or the steps we need to take care of any problem, big or small.

What did I learn?

No matter what we go through, God knows what is best for us in all situations.

Forgive Like God

Scripture: "And when you stand praying, if you hold anything against anyone, forgive him, so that your Father in heaven may forgive you your sins."

- Mark 11:25

God tells us that it's ok to be upset or disappointed about a situation. Still, we shouldn't keep ourselves in a bad mood forever!

One of God's own biggest virtues is His forgiveness. Above all, God knows He did not make us completely perfect and chooses to be patient, forgiving us for our mistakes when we ask Him to. You might remember

Jesus talking a lot about forgiveness from your studies too!

Even when we are upset or get mad at somebody else, when they apologize and ask for our forgiveness, God tells us that He wishes for us to work hard to forgive them and look forward to the future!

What did I learn?

Forgiving others can be hard but never impossible. God asks us to forgive just like we have been forgiven.

No More Fighting!

Scripture: "But now you must also rid yourselves of all such things as these: anger, rage, malice, slander, and filthy language from your lips."

— Colossians 3:8

Fights are no fun for anybody. When a fight happens, instead of the exciting action shots that we get from tv and movies, we often feel upset with those we care about, and even ourselves.

God understands that we make mistakes, and one of the biggest mistakes that lead to fighting is misunderstandings. When we are upset, it can be harder for us to explain what we need help to fix. If we aren't careful, it can cause a huge misunderstanding, especially when we don't mean it!

God doesn't like fighting at all and even tells us that He wants us to keep from fighting each other! His wisdom also shows us that it can be harder to solve our problems through fighting, especially when we hurt each other in the process.

What did I learn?

God doesn't want us to fight! Fighting and anger don't help us walk in God's vision and can keep us from thinking clearly.

Be Rumor Free

Scripture: "Do not go about spreading slander among your people. 'Do not do anything that endangers your neighbor's life. I am the Lord."

- Leviticus 19:16

Have you ever played a game of telephone? You and a few friends gather in a circle in the game. Next, one person starts by whispering a phrase, word, or 'secret' to the person next to them. This 'secret' is passed down the line, and once it returns to the friend who started the game, the words or meaning can change entirely!

Although the telephone is a fun game to make silly sentences, this is how rumors work too. As gossip passes along, it can easily turn into something bad or even harmful if we're not careful!

As we talk with our friends and family, God warns us to not be involved in rumors spreading or talking poorly of others. Mean rumors can hurt, so we should always speak kindly and wisely as God asks us to!

What did I learn?

Spreading rumors can be hurtful and even dangerous…God teaches us not to gossip in all situations.

Sharing Sadness With God

Through the sad and the glad times, God is with us every step of the way. Whenever we feel down, God asks us to share our thoughts. That way, He can help make it better!

In heaven and on earth, God offers us peace and comfort through any time that may be challenging. God understands that we can sometimes feel discouraged, but He also wants us to overcome our challenges through Him.

The next time you feel sad or upset, turn to God for help and let him know. This way, He can help us through anything we might need help with.

What did I learn?

God is with us through happy times and sad ones. With Him, we can share our sadness and be uplifted.

God is a Healer

Scripture: "Heal me, O Lord, and I will be healed; save me and I will be saved, for you are the one I praise."

- Jeremiah 17:14

Every day, there are so many ways God helps us! From taking care of our feelings to ensuring we have the things we need, God is our greatest healer in both our spirit and body.

Many stories in the Bible show just how much God cares about healing his children. Through God, there are even tales of Jesus performing healing miracles, curing the blind, and relieving others in pain.

Regardless, God is a proven healer for many wounds, including those we cannot see. He gives us rest, time, and guidance to improve from anything that stands in our way!

What did I learn?

From the smallest worries to the biggest pains, God can heal and help all things!

God Knows You!

Scripture: "I am the good shepherd; I know my sheep and my sheep know me."

- John 10:14

From the vast oceans and forests to the tiniest microscopic critters, it's no secret that God has created every little part of our lives, But do you know just how much He knows you, too?

As our creator, God has not only had a plan for us throughout our time until we return to heaven, but He is very familiar with every part of us, big and small!

We are all created to God's wishes inside and out. Just as He sees our outside features, God notices all dreams and goals that we wish for deep down!

Just as we know God very well and continue to learn about Him, we can rest assured that God will never misunderstand us. He pays close attention to us and, as our creator, knows us very well!

What did I learn?

From the hairs on our heads to our greatest wishes and dreams, God knows us from head to toe!

God Always Helps

Scripture: "Behold, God is my helper; the Lord is the upholder of my life."

- Psalm 54:4

No matter where we are or what we are doing, we can always rely on God being one of our biggest helpers!

Just as God asks us to help and be generous in many ways, from spreading his word to never being greedy, God acts in generosity too! Wherever we are, we can rely on God to lend a helping hand, even if it's in spirit, because he truly cares about us!

Finally, God has many ways of being our biggest helper. Sometimes God might pair us up and help through another person, as He has done through Noah, Moses, and countless other leaders in the Bible. Other times, He shows us how our strength can be found from within by guiding us through our own ideas after prayer. God works in many different ways to ensure we get the help we need, just as He expects us to do for others when we can.

What did I learn?

No matter our challenges, God will be our biggest helper in all we do!

Be a Strong Leader

Scripture: "God is our refuge and strength, a very present help in trouble."

- Psalm 46:1

There are plenty of opportunities to be leaders in our homes, school, or community, but what do you think it means to be a strong leader?

At certain times in our lives, God may call us to be leaders and share our knowledge or expertise with others. Other times, He may ask us to follow another person's lead too, but in all cases, He works hard to help keep our leadership strong no matter what.

Finally, being a strong leader for God can mean many things! Instead of just being strong with our muscles, the strength of a good leader can come in many different forms, like understanding a specific subject or even seeking God's guidance to solve big plans! No matter how we find our leadership strengths, He will surely help guide us confidently.

What did I learn?

Sometimes, God calls us to be leaders in sharing His ideas. We should always work hard to be strong leaders!

God is Limitless

Scripture: "Great is our Lord and mighty in power; his understanding has no limit."

- Psalms 147:5

Imagine a person that has the superpower to do anything and everything. From solving every single problem to ensuring everything was operating smoothly. It would be a huge, nearly impossible responsibility for us to think of doing it. Still, it is easy for God to do it!

The strength and power of God can be hard to understand because He is truly limitless! From the biggest worries to the smallest, He is with us at all times and with every single person and creation on earth.

God is the greatest creator as well. His limitless abilities have created such a vast, varied world that we still discover new animals and areas we've never reached. With all of this, there's no doubt that God is truly limitless in what He can do!

What did I learn?

God is limitless in what He can do for us. He has no boundaries, and through him, all is possible!

When in Doubt, Pray!

Scripture: "So I say to you: Ask and it will be given to you; seek and you will find; knock and the door will be opened to you."

- Luke 11:9

Sometimes you might feel hopeful, and others when you feel discouraged. Whenever you have doubts about yourself, your situation, or others, what is something you can always do? Pray!

If you're feeling down or doubtful, praying to God and sharing your feelings with him can have a lot of benefits. God is a great listener and problem solver, so there's no better guide for any doubts.

When we pray and share our feelings, of course, it might take some time for God to answer our prayers, but He always listens to us no matter what, and you will start to feel the weight of your worries start to lift away.

What did I learn?

Whenever we feel down or need guidance, we can always lean on God by asking for His help through prayer.

Grow With God

Scripture: "But grow in the grace and knowledge of our Lord and Savior Jesus Christ. To him be glory both now and forever! Amen"

- Peter 3:18

No matter where we go or what we see, we should grow our lives with God!

God helps us in so many ways in our lives. He helps us with our present worries and takes care of any others we might think of for the future. We should continue to seek His guidance as we grow in all that we do.

Maintaining a good relationship with God is important for many parts of our lives. God often helps us in countless ways, growing our minds, body, and spirit to be strong in goodness for the rest of our lives. He also allows us to share our experiences of His blessings and lessons with others!

What did I learn?

God helps us grow in our minds, body, and spirit.

Stay Positive!

Good and bad things can happen as we go about our day, but with God, we can always focus on the good!

God understands that we might not always be cheerful or experience fun things. Even so, in many smaller problems, we can look to God for the bright side and make our day positive.

Imagine you had a good day at school, but by the end of the day found out that you didn't do very well on your last quiz. It can be discouraging news to hear! Fortunately, we have plenty of chances to fix it, so you shouldn't let it make your whole day bad!

Like this example, God often gives us many chances to improve a bad situation. Sometimes if we look at the big picture with gratitude for all that is good in our lives, the bad parts will look much smaller!

What did I learn?

God always hopes to uplift us and keep our spirits positive in all situations!

Who are God's Angels?

Did you know that you have guardian angels watching over you? God's angels work hard to ensure you are okay, just like He does!

God's angels have a lot of jobs. A long time ago, God created angels to care for everything on earth just as He does. Angels live in heaven with God but are unique in how they can help share important information between heaven and earth. In the bible, angels follow God's rules by having a big role in sharing messages and keeping us safe!

Wherever they are, God's angels help to keep away all bad things from us. They always choose to work in all that is good. Some think angels may even help share the messages we are sending to God when we pray!

What did I learn?

God's angels do a lot for God. They are warriors and protectors for all that follow His word.

Who is Moses?

Scripture: "Moses returned to the LORD and said, 'O Lord, why have you brought trouble upon these people? Is this why you sent me?'"

- Exodus 5:22

The story of Moses is one of bravery, loyalty, and freedom! As one of the most well-known prophets who followed God, many know Moses' name, but why is he so important?

When Moses was a baby, life was dangerous! He had to begin his journey traveling from a basket on the Nile river to escape danger. Later, when he was older, he even had to leave where he grew up in Egypt because of the threats to his people.

Fortunately, long ago, God chose to call out to Moses, giving him a big job; to free the rest of God's people from Israel and lead them to safety through deserts and oceans.

It was a challenge that Moses was not sure he could do, but he left his faith in God's plans and was blessed with success!

What did I learn?

Moses had a big job from God; He had to ensure all God's people could travel safely away from their enemies!

ADISAN Publishing AB

www.ingramcontent.com/pod-product-compliance
Lightning Source LLC
Chambersburg PA
CBHW070441160726
48196CB00083B/368